HAL•LEONARD

JAZZ PLAY-ALONG®

ok and CD for B♭, E♭, C and Bass Clef Instruments

volume 174

Tin Pan Alley

Arranged by Mark Taylor

Produced by Jim Roberts, Craig Fraedrich, and Paul Murtha

T0081576

BOOK

CD

ISBN 978-1-4803-4155-5

HAL•LEONARD®
CORPORATION
7777 W. BLUEMOUND RD. P.O. BOX 13819 MILWAUKEE, WI 53213

In Australia Contact:
Hal Leonard Australia Pty. Ltd.
4 Lentara Court
Cheltenham, Victoria, 3192 Australia
Email: ausadmin@halleonard.com.au

Visit Hal Leonard Online at
www.halleonard.com

TIN PAN ALLEY

Volume 174

Arranged by Mark Taylor
Produced by Jim Roberts, Craig Fraedrich, and Paul Murtha

Featured Players:

Graham Breedlove–Trumpet
John Desalme–Tenor and Clarinet
Tony Nalker–Piano
Jim Roberts–Guitar
Paul Henry–Bass
Todd Harrison–Drums

**Recorded at Bias Studios, Springfield, Virginia
Bob Dawson, Engineer**

HOW TO USE THE CD:

Each song has two tracks:

1) Split Track/Melody

Woodwind, Brass, Keyboard, and **Mallet Players** can use this track as a learning tool for melody style and inflection.

Bass Players can learn and perform with this track – remove the recorded bass track by turning down the volume on the LEFT channel.

Keyboard and **Guitar Players** can learn and perform with this track – remove the recorded piano part by turning down the volume on the RIGHT channel.

2) Full Stereo Track

Soloists or **Groups** can learn and perform with this accompaniment track with the RHYTHM SECTION only.

PRETTY BABY

WORDS BY GUS KAHN
MUSIC BY EGBERT VAN ALSTYNE AND TONY JACKSON

CD
5 : SPLIT TRACK/MELODY
6 : FULL STEREO TRACK

C VERSION

THE DARKTOWN STRUTTERS' BALL

CD
13 : SPLIT TRACK/MELODY
14 : FULL STEREO TRACK

WORDS AND MUSIC BY
SHELTON BROOKS

C VERSION

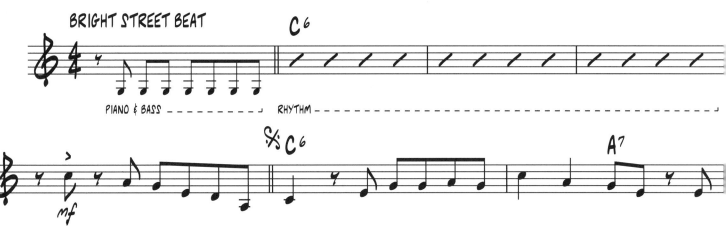

FOR ME AND MY GAL

WORDS BY EDGAR LESLIE AND E. RAY GOETZ
MUSIC BY GEORGE W. MEYER

CD
3 : SPLIT TRACK/MELODY
4 : FULL STEREO TRACK

C VERSION

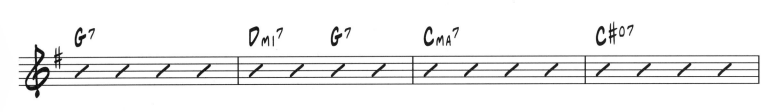

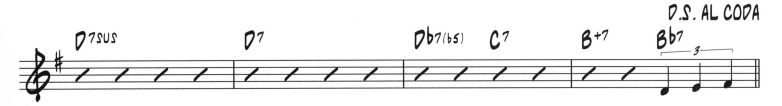

CD

9 : SPLIT TRACK/MELODY
10 : FULL STEREO TRACK

SMILES

WORDS BY J. WILL CALLAHAN
MUSIC BY LEE S. ROBERTS

C VERSION

MEDIUM BOSSA

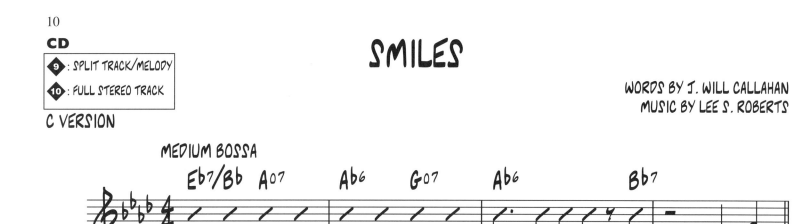

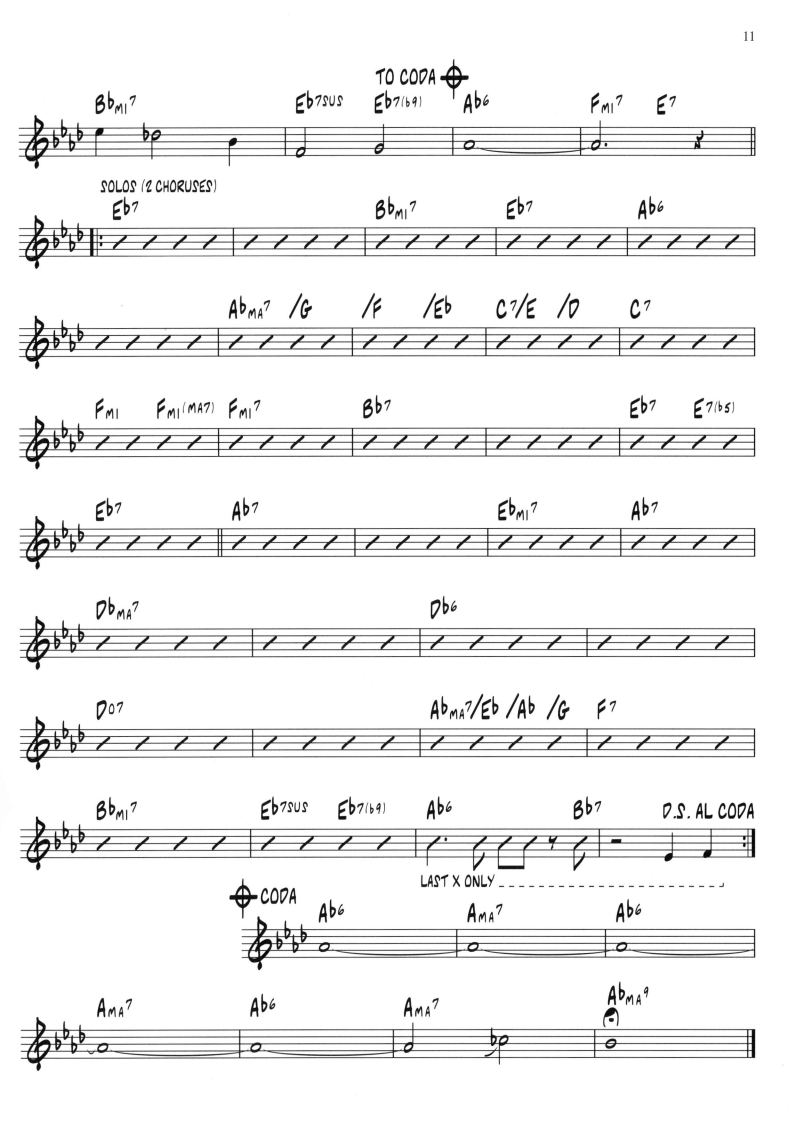

SOMEBODY STOLE MY GAL

CD
11 : SPLIT TRACK/MELODY
12 : FULL STEREO TRACK

WORDS AND MUSIC BY
LEO WOOD

C VERSION

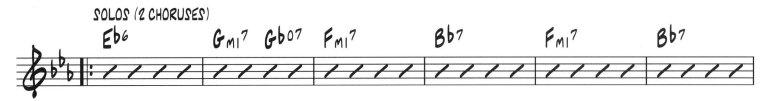

CD
⑮ : SPLIT TRACK/MELODY
⑯ : FULL STEREO TRACK

C VERSION

TOOT, TOOT, TOOTSIE!
(GOOD-BYE!)

WORDS AND MUSIC BY GUS KAHN, ERNIE ERDMAN,
DAN RUSSO AND TED FIORITO

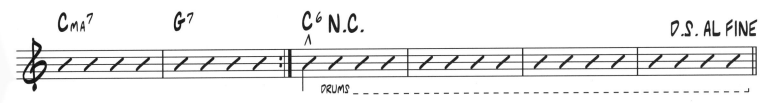

CD

17 : SPLIT TRACK/MELODY
18 : FULL STEREO TRACK

C VERSION

WHILE STROLLING THROUGH
THE PARK ONE DAY

WORDS AND MUSIC BY ED HALEY
AND ROBERT A. KEISER

MEDIUM JAZZ WALTZ

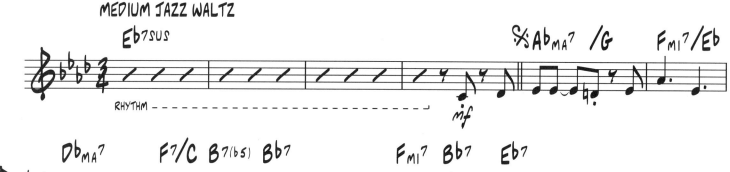

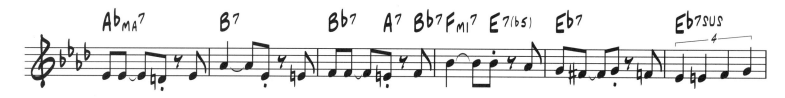

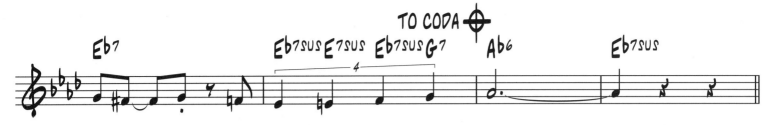

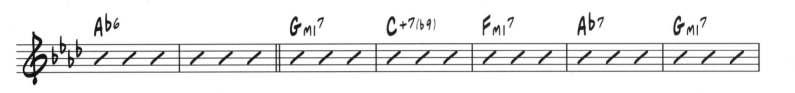

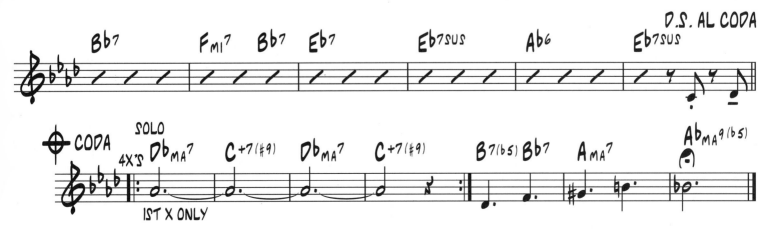

CD

YOU MADE ME LOVE YOU
(I DIDN'T WANT TO DO IT)

WORDS BY JOE McCARTHY
MUSIC BY JAMES V. MONACO

C VERSION

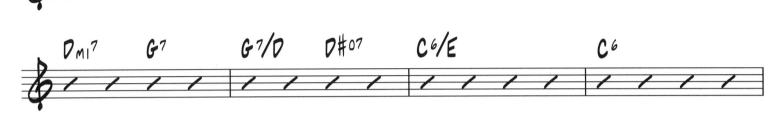

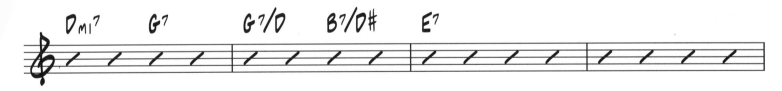

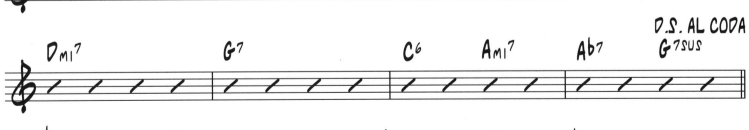

SHINE ON, HARVEST MOON

WORDS BY JACK NORWORTH
MUSIC BY NORA BAYES AND JACK NORWORTH

SHINE ON, HARVEST MOON

WORDS BY JACK NORWORTH
MUSIC BY NORA BAYES AND JACK NORWORTH

Bb VERSION

BY THE LIGHT OF THE SILVERY MOON

PRETTY BABY

WORDS BY GUS KAHN
MUSIC BY EGBERT VAN ALSTYNE AND TONY JACKSON

CD
5: SPLIT TRACK/MELODY
6: FULL STEREO TRACK

Bb VERSION
MEDIUM SWING

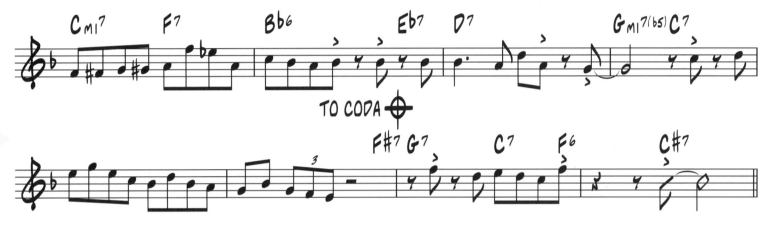

SOLOS (3 CHORUSES)

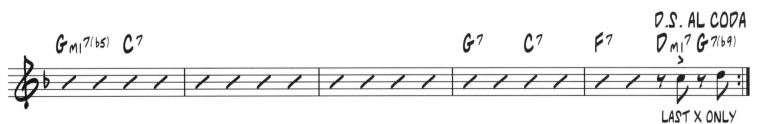

CD

13 : SPLIT TRACK/MELODY
14 : FULL STEREO TRACK

THE DARKTOWN STRUTTERS' BALL

WORDS AND MUSIC BY
SHELTON BROOKS

Bb VERSION

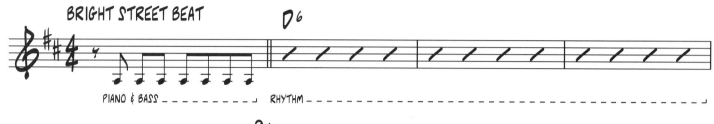

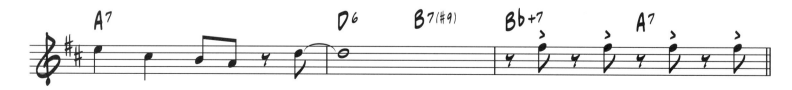

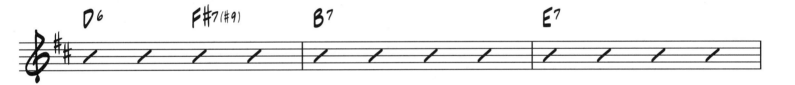

FOR ME AND MY GAL

WORDS BY EDGAR LESLIE AND E. RAY GOETZ
MUSIC BY GEORGE W. MEYER

Bb VERSION

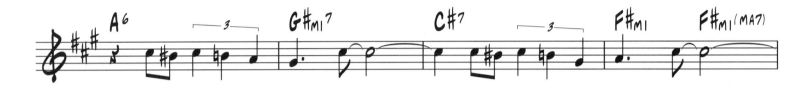

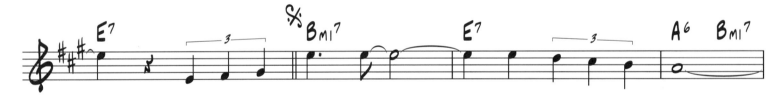

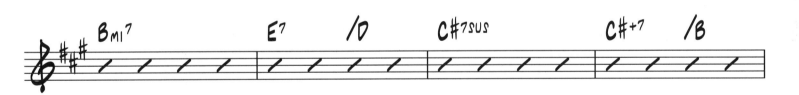

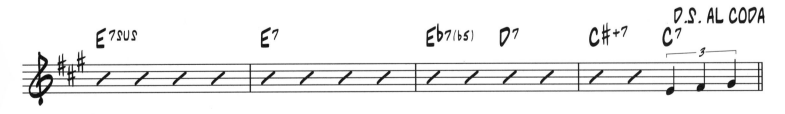

CD

◆ 9 : SPLIT TRACK/MELODY
◆ 10 : FULL STEREO TRACK

SMILES

WORDS BY J. WILL CALLAHAN
MUSIC BY LEE S. ROBERTS

Bb VERSION

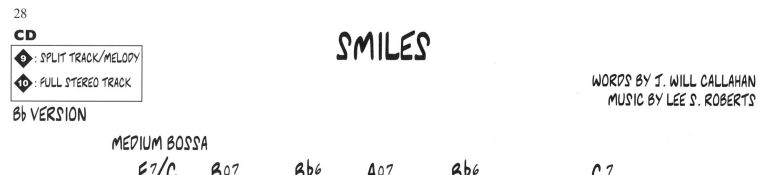

MEDIUM BOSSA

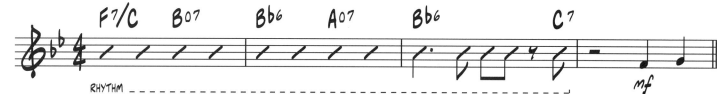

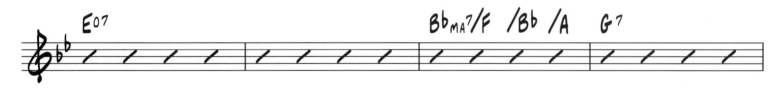

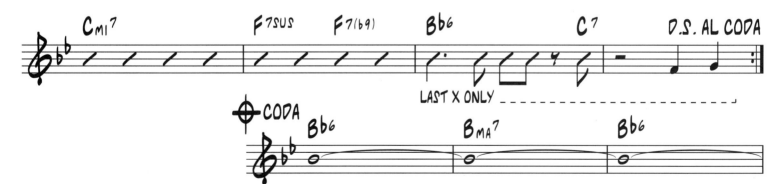

SOMEBODY STOLE MY GAL

WORDS AND MUSIC BY
LEO WOOD

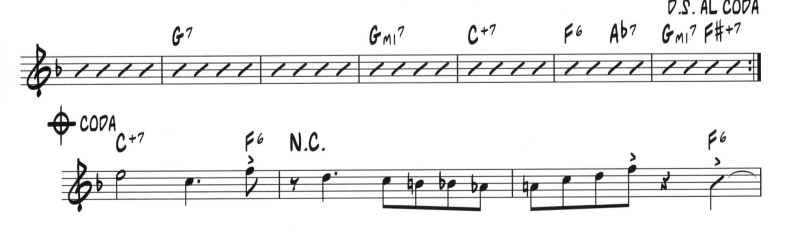

CD

15 : SPLIT TRACK/MELODY
16 : FULL STEREO TRACK

Bb VERSION

TOOT, TOOT, TOOTSIE!
(GOOD-BYE!)

WORDS AND MUSIC BY GUS KAHN, ERNIE ERDMAN,
DAN RUSSO AND TED FIORITO

WHILE STROLLING THROUGH THE PARK ONE DAY

WORDS AND MUSIC BY ED HALEY
AND ROBERT A. KEISER

CD
17 : SPLIT TRACK/MELODY
18 : FULL STEREO TRACK

Bb VERSION

MEDIUM JAZZ WALTZ

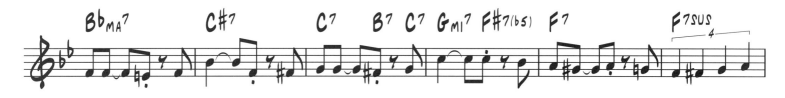

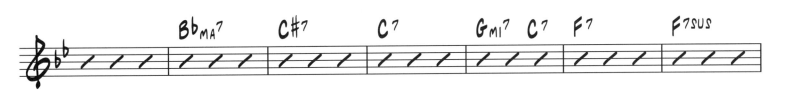

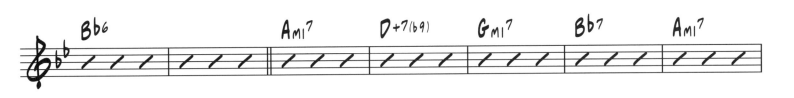

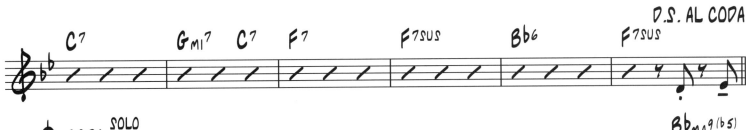

CD
19: SPLIT TRACK/MELODY
20: FULL STEREO TRACK

YOU MADE ME LOVE YOU
(I DIDN'T WANT TO DO IT)

WORDS BY JOE MCCARTHY
MUSIC BY JAMES V. MONACO

Bb VERSION

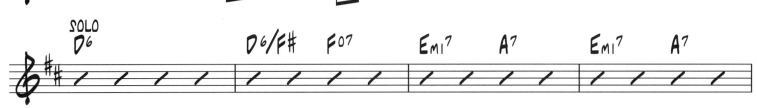

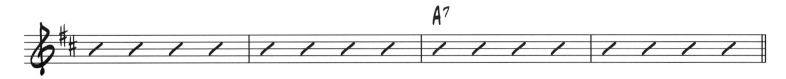

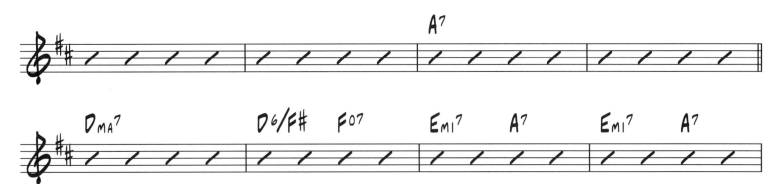

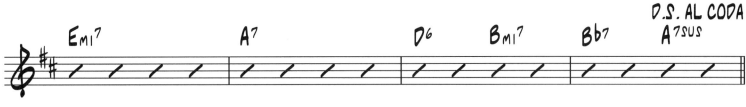

BY THE LIGHT OF THE SILVERY MOON

LYRICS BY ED MADDEN
MUSIC BY GUS EDWARDS

PRETTY BABY

CD
⑤ : SPLIT TRACK/MELODY
⑥ : FULL STEREO TRACK

Eb VERSION

WORDS BY GUS KAHN
MUSIC BY EGBERT VAN ALSTYNE AND TONY JACKSON

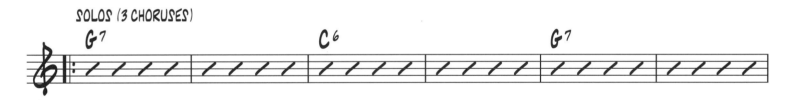

CD

13 : SPLIT TRACK/MELODY
14 : FULL STEREO TRACK

THE DARKTOWN STRUTTERS' BALL

WORDS AND MUSIC BY
SHELTON BROOKS

Eb VERSION

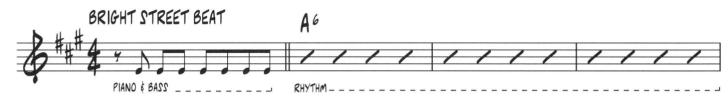

FOR ME AND MY GAL

WORDS BY EDGAR LESLIE AND E. RAY GOETZ
MUSIC BY GEORGE W. MEYER

CD
- ◆**3** : SPLIT TRACK/MELODY
- ◆**4** : FULL STEREO TRACK

Eb VERSION

MEDIUM BOSSA

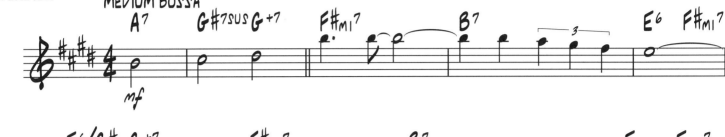

TO CODA ⊕

SOLO

F#mi7 | B7 | E6　F#mi7 | E6/G#　G+7

F#mi7 | B7 | E　Ema7 | E6

D#mi7 | G#7 | C#mi　C#mi(ma7) | C#mi7

F#7 | | B7　Cma7 | B7

F#mi7 | B7 | E6　F#mi7 | E6/G#　G+7

F#mi7 | B7　/A | G#7sus | G#+7　/F#

E7 | Bmi7　E7 | Ama7 | A#o7

D.S. AL CODA

B7sus | B7 | Bb7(b5)　A7 | G#+7　G7

CODA　Bb7(b5)　A7　　G#+7(#9)　A7　　Bb7(b5)　F7(b5)　　Ema7(b5)

3X'S

1ST X ONLY

CD

◆ 9 : SPLIT TRACK/MELODY
◆ 10 : FULL STEREO TRACK

SMILES

WORDS BY J. WILL CALLAHAN
MUSIC BY LEE S. ROBERTS

E♭ VERSION

SOMEBODY STOLE MY GAL

CD
11 : SPLIT TRACK/MELODY
12 : FULL STEREO TRACK

WORDS AND MUSIC BY
LEO WOOD

Eb VERSION

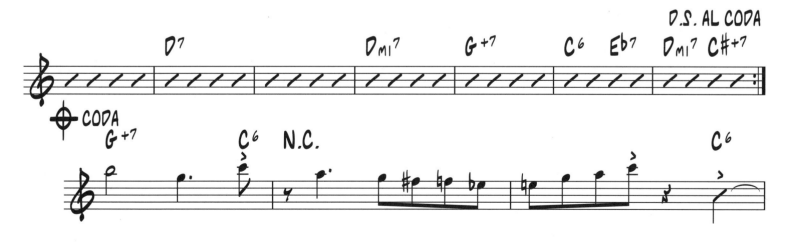

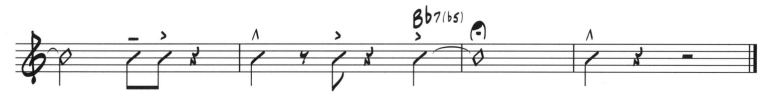

CD

17 : SPLIT TRACK/MELODY
18 : FULL STEREO TRACK

Eb VERSION

WHILE STROLLING THROUGH
THE PARK ONE DAY

WORDS AND MUSIC BY ED HALEY
AND ROBERT A. KEISER

MEDIUM JAZZ WALTZ

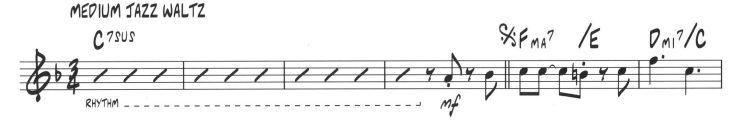

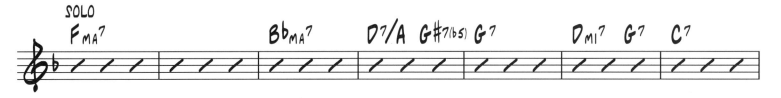

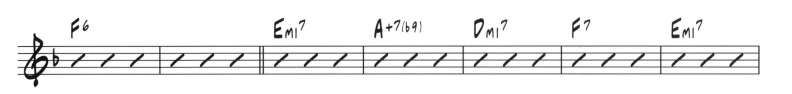

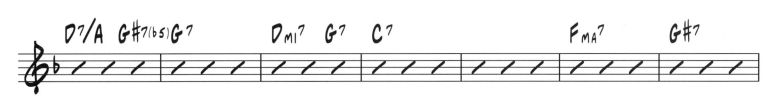

YOU MADE ME LOVE YOU
(I DIDN'T WANT TO DO IT)

WORDS BY JOE McCARTHY
MUSIC BY JAMES V. MONACO

Eb VERSION

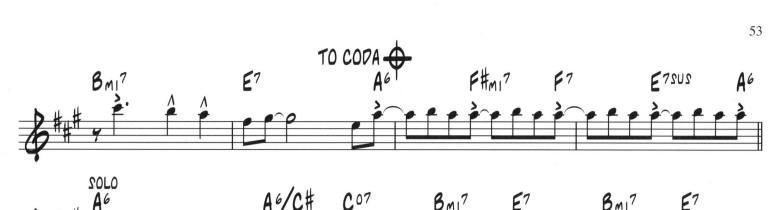

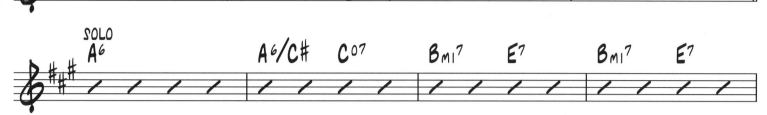

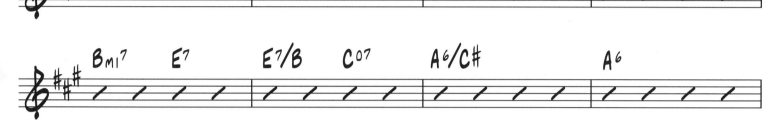

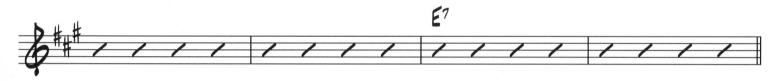

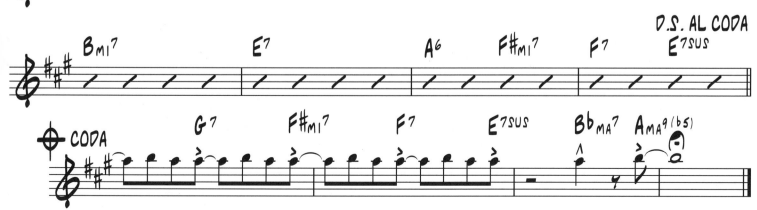

SHINE ON, HARVEST MOON

WORDS BY JACK NORWORTH
MUSIC BY NORA BAYES AND JACK NORWORTH

Eb VERSION

SHINE ON, HARVEST MOON

WORDS BY JACK NORWORTH
MUSIC BY NORA BAYES AND JACK NORWORTH

BY THE LIGHT OF THE SILVERY MOON

LYRICS BY ED MADDEN
MUSIC BY GUS EDWARDS

PRETTY BABY

WORDS BY GUS KAHN
MUSIC BY EGBERT VAN ALSTYNE AND TONY JACKSON

CD
5 : SPLIT TRACK/MELODY
6 : FULL STEREO TRACK

♩: C VERSION

THE DARKTOWN STRUTTERS' BALL

WORDS AND MUSIC BY
SHELTON BROOKS

CD
13 : SPLIT TRACK/MELODY
14 : FULL STEREO TRACK

𝄢 : C VERSION

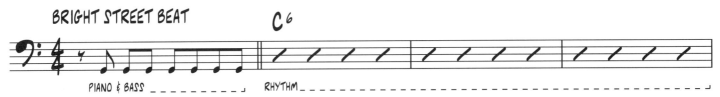

BRIGHT STREET BEAT

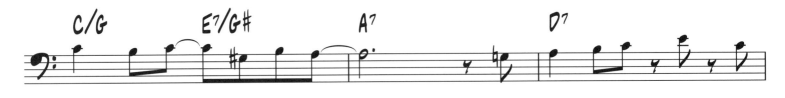

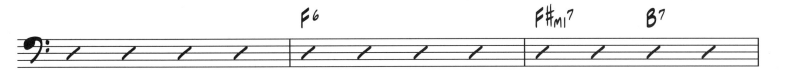

FOR ME AND MY GAL

WORDS BY EDGAR LESLIE AND E. RAY GOETZ
MUSIC BY GEORGE W. MEYER

CD
3 : SPLIT TRACK/MELODY
4 : FULL STEREO TRACK

⑨: C VERSION

SMILES

WORDS BY J. WILL CALLAHAN
MUSIC BY LEE S. ROBERTS

CD
9 : SPLIT TRACK/MELODY
10 : FULL STEREO TRACK

C VERSION

SOLOS (2 CHORUSES)

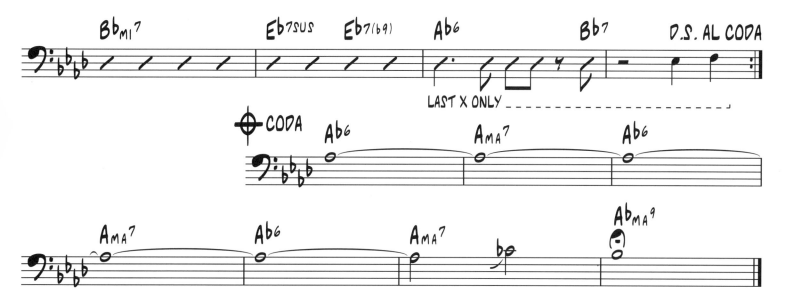

SOMEBODY STOLE MY GAL

WORDS AND MUSIC BY
LEO WOOD

CD

11 : SPLIT TRACK/MELODY
12 : FULL STEREO TRACK

𝄢: C VERSION

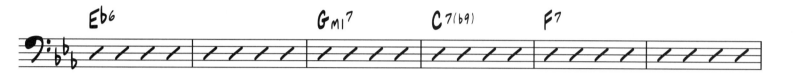

CD

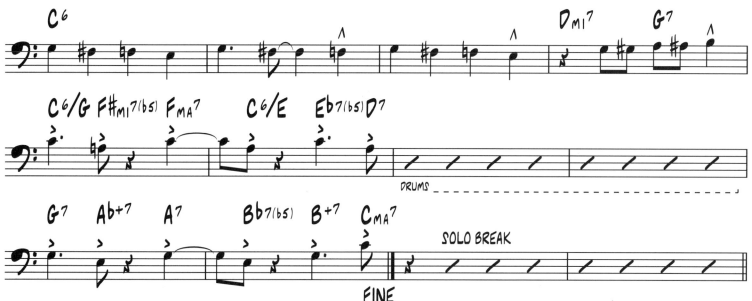

CD

: SPLIT TRACK/MELODY
: FULL STEREO TRACK

𝄢: C VERSION

WHILE STROLLING THROUGH
THE PARK ONE DAY

WORDS AND MUSIC BY ED HALEY
AND ROBERT A. KEISER

MEDIUM JAZZ WALTZ

YOU MADE ME LOVE YOU
(I DIDN'T WANT TO DO IT)

🎵: C VERSION

WORDS BY JOE MCCARTHY
MUSIC BY JAMES V. MONACO

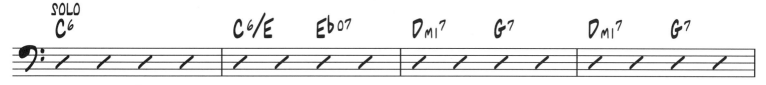

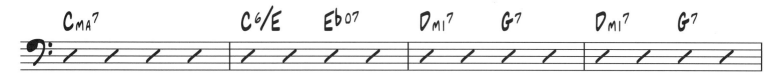

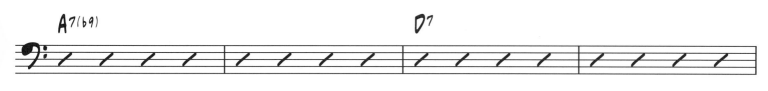

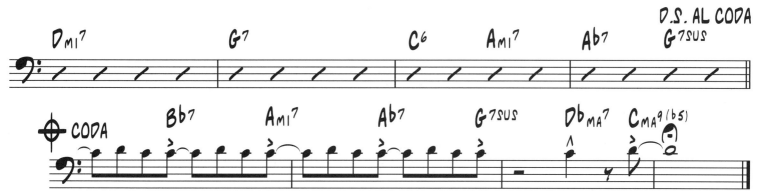

Presenting the Hal Leonard JAZZ PLAY-ALONG® SERIES

For use with all B-flat, E-flat, Bass Clef and C instruments, the Jazz Play-Along® Series is the ultimate learning tool for all jazz musicians. With musician-friendly lead sheets, melody cues, and other split-track choices on the included CD, these first-of-a-kind packages help you master improvisation while playing some of the greatest tunes of all time. FOR STUDY, each tune includes a split track with: melody cue with proper style and inflection • professional rhythm tracks • choruses for soloing • removable bass part • removable piano part. FOR PERFORMANCE, each tune also has: an additional full stereo accompaniment track (no melody) • additional choruses for soloing.